All About T

Cont

Special thanks to TETRA (UK) LTD
for help in compiling this book.

Introduction

The care of tropical fish can be a complex subject, and it is easy to forget the simple pleasures of keeping and watching fish, and become immersed in all the technicalities of water chemistry and equipment.

This book will help you get involved in the hobby by keeping a few basic tropical fish. After that, further reading and experience can open up a world of fishkeeping opportunities.

You may already have kept hardy freshwater fish, like goldfish, in a simple unfiltered tank, with few problems. But tropical fish require just a little more care, and some extra equipment. Before we look at some of the reasons why this care and equipment are important, let us establish two points.

- Tropical fish vary a great deal in their needs, size, and behaviour. What is right for one species may be totally wrong for another.
- There is very often more than one way of keeping tropical fish properly. A great many 'experts' have strong views on fish care, and in the end, you must listen to them, read magazines and books, visit shops and make up your own mind.

In this simple account of the hobby, the aim is to get you up and running with an aquarium that will successfully maintain a basic community of tropicals.

Fishkeeping is an absorbing hobby, but it is wise to start off with a basic set-up and learn how to care for your fish properly.

The Elements

Why Water Matters...

Water is the single most important element in fishkeeping, and especially tropical fishkeeping.

The vast majority of the coldwater fish we keep – Koi and goldfish, for instance – come from middle-of-the-road lowland waters where the acidity varies but is usually somewhere near neutral (pH7), and the temperatures may vary from 60 to 80 degrees F (15 - 27 C). This is handy as the water that comes out of most taps will be suitable for immediate use – once the chlorine is removed with a tap water conditioner, or by bubbling it off with an airstone.

The Environment

Natural conditions around the world vary hugely, and influence the make-up of the water that tropical fish swim in. Over millions of years fish have adapted to live in some

Temperature control and monitoring the acidity (pH) level of the water are the essential elements of tropical fishkeeping.

unlikely settings, such as sunless underground caves and sulphur springs.

A female Siamese fighting fish.

However, most of the tropical fish we keep come from jungle settings, and from rivers and streams fed by high mountain ranges like the Andes. Water flowing off these mountains is quite acid. The rocks that the water falls off are hard and inert, and do not add anything to the water. In the jungle, rotting vegetation makes the water even more acid.

Many fish from South America, West Africa, and South East Asia are found in quite acid waters (but never assume that's the case – always ask about the fish you want, or read up on it before purchasing).

Brochis

Despite this, most of the tropical fish in your local shop will come from fish farms where they will all have been raised in a higher pH than their natural homes and will be very adaptable to the pH of the water, especially if it is around neutral (pH7). More important is maintaining a temperature of at least 70F (21C) or higher – up to 80F (27C) in some cases.

The problem comes with wild-caught fish, which may have come from quite acid waters (South American Discus) or quite hard waters (Rift Lake cichlids from Africa), and will need the same water conditions in your tank. They may also prefer higher temperatures (Discus), or slightly lower ones (Golden barbs), or they may be used to widely-varying temperatures (White Cloud Mountain minnows).

Therefore, it is probably best to start tropical fishkeeping with either a community of small, attractive and adaptable commercially-bred fish, or with one or two of the larger, hardier species which have lots of character. Both will be undemanding and live happily in almost everyone's tapwater.

pH Testing

When testing the acidity (pH) of the water, you may well discover that water comes out of your tap at one level of acidity, and after a day or two it has become more acid. This is because many water companies have to add 'temporary hardness' to the tapwater to protect the pipes.

For this reason, it is important to store water for a few days before adding it to your tank. This will eliminate the chlorine which will naturally dissipate after a few days. Chlorine protects *you* against bacteria in the water but does fish no good at all. A stronger version, chloramine, can even poison your fish after it breaks down. Many fishkeepers now use a commercial dechlorinator to protect their fish against these and other nasties in the tapwater. Some owners of sensitive fish even purchase special tapwater filters to remove a wide range of pollutants.

A pH test kit.

Dechlorinators are used by some fishkeepers to reduce the chlorine level in the water.

What Is A Tropical Fish?

The Internal Structure

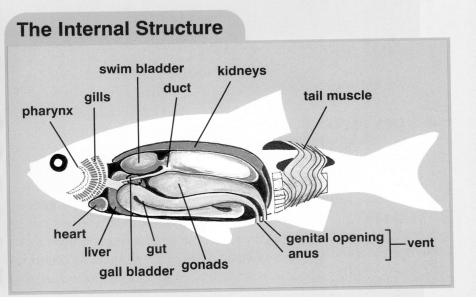

So What Is A Tropical Fish?

Good question. The greatest delight of tropical fish is their sheer numbers and diversity.

A simple answer might be that it is a fish that requires a heater in the tank to keep properly. But some fish that are commonly listed as tropical will survive in cooler temperatures similar to those suitable to goldfish. White Cloud Mountain minnows are the classic example – quite happy at 65F (18C).

The 'average' tropical fish will be happiest at temperatures between 68F and 80F (20C and 27C). A temperature of 76F (24C) is a good compromise.

The tropics, of course, is the zone between the tropics of Capricorn and Cancer (the equator in the middle). Traditionally this is the warmest part of the earth, and most tropical fish (not surprisingly) are found in this vast region.

What Is A Tropical Fish?

Characteristics

The tropical fish we can keep vary enormously in size, from the minute Mosquito fish and other miniatures up to the six-foot long Red-tail catfish, which really demands an indoor heated pond.

What do they eat? There are vegetarians, omnivores and out-and-out predatory carnivores in their ranks. Obviously you need to know something about their feeding habits to get the right mix of fish.

Most breed by laying eggs, some scattering them willy-nilly, some building nests, others elaborately concealing and guarding their young. Those that don't lay eggs may conceal their young inside their bodies and give birth to live offspring.

Green sailfin molly

Discus: the variety of tropical fish is staggering.

The Families

Among the popular tropical aquarium fish there are dominant families and groups.

X-ray tetra

• Many of the popular tropical starter fish are found among the barbs, rasboras and characins.

Guppy

• Others, such as guppies and platies, are usually classed simply as livebearers.

• Catfish come from hundreds of genera. They are always popular, but not all are suitable for beginners.

Plecostomus catfish

Koi angel

• For more advanced fishkeepers, there are the many cichlid species.

• Very large, often solitary species are called oddballs or tankbusters. This group of unrelated species includes giant vegetarians like the Osphronemus gourami and predators like the Snakehead family. Later on, we will choose some good starter fish from this huge range of possibilities.

Essential Equipment

You may have kept goldfish and other coldwater species in a pond or tank without much equipment. To keep tropicals, you will need a few essentials.

Aquarium

Buy the biggest you can afford in glass or acrylic, but never smaller than 24 ins x 12 ins x 12 ins (12 US gallons/48 litres). The bigger the aquarium, the more stable it will be in water chemistry and temperature.

Tanks come in a variety of shapes and sizes, but the best plan is to buy the biggest you can afford.

Filter

You need a filter to keep your fish alive. The favourite system for newcomers to British fishkeeping using smaller tanks is probably the internal power filter. There are many reliable makes, but all consist of a box with a sponge inside, and slots in it. On top of the box, a sealed (electrically-safe) pump sits and sucks water through the sponge before pumping it back into the tank. These filters often offer other refinements, such as features that aerate the water too.

Tropical fish come from a wide range of habitats.

External Filter

In the USA small external hang-on filters are the filter of choice on smaller tanks. Not all British tanks (especially the tank hoods) are adapted to use these filters and they are not widely available, but they are excellent. They offer a variety of media, and as they are above the tank and out of the main body of water, they provide excellent aeration of the filter bacteria and the water that is returned to the tank.

Internal Filter

The undergravel filter remains in favour on some smaller tanks in the UK and larger ones in the USA. In this system a 3-inch layer of gravel is laid over a plate which covers all (or part) of the tank base, and water is sucked through it, either by placing a pump or pumps on uplift tubes, or by putting airstones down these tubes. As the air bubbles up, it drags water with it and, consequently, the water in the main tank, down through the undergravel filter, which makes an excellent home for their bacteria. To work well they must be kept very clean.

> *TIP: By using a filter to pump water DOWN the uplift tubes you can put the undergravel into 'reverse-flow' thereby pushing water up through the gravel and trapping little or no wastes.*

Choosing Equipment

Heater

A heater with a built-in thermostat keeps the water at a constant temperature. You set it, often by trial and error, to the right temperature, usually using a knob on top of a long glass or plastic tube that contains the heater element. Match the power of the heater to the size of your tank.

Now, you could stop here. Nobody actually needs lighting in their tank, except, of course, to see the fish, unless they want to grow plants – (see pages 24 and 25). So, with the addition of a lid of some type to prevent evaporation, fish jumping out, and airborne nasties getting in, you can stop spending. However, you may need or want all or some of the following...

A heater with a built-in thermostat maintains the correct temperature.

Tank Hood And Lighting

The best type is a combined hood and light unit. Many of them are more or less waterproof and they are very safe. If you think you will be in the hobby a long time, choose a hood with room for two or more fluorescent tubes as this is a more flexible arrangement when (for instance) growing plants.

Fluorescent tubes come in various colours and powers. Some are designed to make your fish look good, others to help plants grow, while some are dedicated to matching sunlight or even imitating moonlight. Take advice from your dealer on the best type for your tank.

Beware – fluorescent tubes lose power radically after a year or so and need replacing. Some types actually stop working when they are worn out, so it is

obvious when to change them.
Reflectors can be bought cheaply and
will improve the performance of your
fluorescent tube.

Silver hatchet

Lighting can change the look of your tank. A reddish tube will colour up some fish beautifully; a blue/white light can make them look washed-out.

Air Pump (plus airline and airstone)

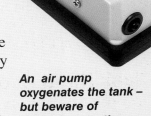

Very warm weather or a heater problem can de-oxygenate your tank water. Small air-powered filters are cheap to buy or easy-to-make, and can be useful in an emergency. Some people find the sight of bubbles in the tank very attractive, too, and bubble displays and air-powered ornaments can be bought.

An air pump oxygenates the tank – but beware of excessive aeration.

Remember that not all fish like living in a jacuzzi and excess aeration may even stress them.

Filter Facts

It is often said that fish swim in their own toilet, and it is true. Fish wastes have nowhere else to go. Everything that can rot in the tank – fish waste, uneaten food, dead fish or plants, even bogwood in the decor – will eventually break down (rot) to produce ammonia, and ammonia is deadly to fish.

In nature, rain dilutes the ammonia, and friendly bacteria break it down to nitrite, also deadly to fish, and then to nitrate which is less dangerous.

Jewel cichlid.

Choosing Equipment

A filter, as its name suggests, filters wastes from the water and makes it *look* clean. However, there is a bonus. The 'friendly' filter bacteria like conditions in the filter system. They fix on its many surfaces, and, using oxygen, convert the wastes in the water as it passes through, breaking down the ammonia, and then breaking down nitrite to nitrate. In a new tank, this bacteria takes time to build up in the filter, which is why you must stock the tank with fish slowly to begin with.

Nitrate is less harmful to your fish, and when you change the water you dilute the nitrate. This is why it is important to carry out routine water changes – just topping up evaporation is not enough. It has been proved that long-term exposure to high nitrate levels is bad for fish.

So change around one-third of your water every fortnight (or a little more if you miss a water change). At the same time, gently wash the sponge of your filter in warm, waste aquarium water – not under the tap as the chlorine kills the invisible bacteria – and not too thoroughly.

Important extras
You will also need:
- Test kits for ammonia and nitrite
- A bucket (the 5-gallon size is most convenient)
- A siphon tube and gravel cleaner for water changes
- Something to scrape off algae (such as a white scouring pad)
- A simple stick-on thermometer
- A net
- Dechlorinator
- A cable tidy to keep wiring neat (choose one with switches for individual items of equipment)
- High-quality flake food.

Nitrite test kit.

Ammonia test kit.

Siphon and tube.

Looking Good

A tank stand or cabinet is a better, safer and more attractive option than placing the tank on a sideboard or table. If the cabinet matches the hood, and both match your other furniture and the decor of the room, so much the better.

You may prefer the natural look when choosing decor.

Backdrop: The back of the tank needs a backdrop. You may prefer the naturalistic photographic planted type, bought on a roll, or a plain blackdrop. You can paint the outside of the back of the tank any colour you wish...

Gravel: A layer of gravel is suggested at the base of the tank. This is available in a huge range of sizes, and in dozens of natural or unnatural colours. Many of the modern gravels are effectively sealed in acrylic and so will not affect your water chemistry. Otherwise, look for natural gravels labelled 'hardness-free'. This should be safe for use with acid-loving fish, should you wish to keep them.

Decor: The inside of the tank needs decor (and so do the fish, you could argue). The range of items available is spectacular – so just a small warning. Even 'safe' decor sold for aquarium use may affect the water in your aquarium. Bogwood and other woods colour the water and can make it more acid. Some real and imitation rocks can make the water harder.

Never grab a rock from the garden or while out walking and put it in the tank. Beware of anything that might have been exposed to sprays or insecticides.

There are plenty of 'fantasy' ornaments to choose from.

Setting Up Your Tank

Locate your tank where you can get the maximum enjoyment from it – but ensure it is out of direct sunlight and free from draughts.

The Location

The first task is to choose the right site for your aquarium. It should be out of direct sunlight and draughts (to avoid heat and algae problems), away from hustle and bustle, but in regular full view so that you can enjoy it. Of course, you need access to electricity.

Choose the size of the aquarium to fit this space. Buy the largest you can afford, with a limit of 4 ft in length – a larger tank requires more elaborate and expensive filtration. Position the stand or cabinet, making sure it is level. Then, if required, place a layer of polystyrene under the tank. Attach or add your chosen backdrop.

Basic Tropical Set-up

Take time to set up your aquarium – you have only one chance of getting it right! Lay out all your equipment, and then follow this step-by-step guide.

1 Position the tank and then filter (this will depend on the type you are using, see page 10). Your heater can either go immediately in this outflow or at the other end of the tank to even out temperatures.

Positioning the tank.

Putting in the gravel.

2 If you are using an internal power filter, a thin layer of gravel to cover the base is all that is required and it will be easy to clean. You may need more gravel if you are going to use plastic plants with bases that have to be buried.

DID YOU KNOW?

Using red lights or tubes with a red cover can allow you to watch nocturnal species, like catfish, after dark. The red light does not seem to bother the fish as they go about their normal lives.

Setting up Your Tank

3 Arrange your chosen decor. Decide what you want in the tank, starting with the fishes' needs – then thinking about what looks good. Some fish may need caves and hiding places, others need lots of swimming space. Some like to hide among real or artificial plants, others want to swim in shoals.

Positioning the decor.

4 Now add the water, using a plate, colander or a spray to make sure it does not move the decor around.

Planting the tank.

Adding the water.

5 If you are using real plants, stop after half-filling the tank and plant them.

6 When the tank is full, add dechlorinator, and turn on the filter.

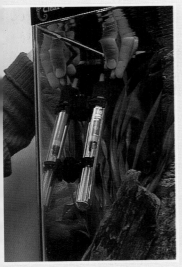

Turn on the thermostat.

7 Let the tank come up to room temperature, then turn on the thermostat. Leave for a couple of days, adjusting the temperature to around 76F – and you are ready to add fish.

8 Put the hood, and condensation tray if any, on the tank – there's no need to turn on the lights yet.

Fitting the lighting system in the hood.

Stocking The Tank

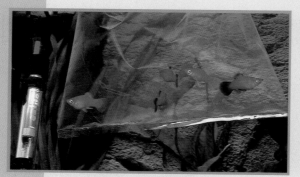

When introducing fish, float the bag for at least 30 minutes.

Everyone wants to buy fish immediately, but resist the temptation – and never add the fish all at once. The bacteria in your filter, as we saw earlier, do not appear instantly; they need to establish themselves gradually.

So wait a day or two to ensure everything is working, then buy two to four hardy tropicals (say one 2-inch fish per foot of tank length) and introduce these first. Good species for this role are platies, Zebra danios, Golden barbs, or Black widow tetras, all of which are hardy.

Add these after floating the bag for up to 30 minutes, and gradually adding water from the tank to the bag.

The First Few Days

Feed the new fish sparingly, once a day. At a different time, do a daily test for ammonia. This will gradually peak then fall. If it gets too high, stop feeding for a day or two, and make a small water change. Next, test for nitrite which should also rise and then fall. When this has happened, do your first big water change and add up to four more fish.

Earlier we mentioned keeping a couple of larger "pet" fish instead of a community tank. In this case you have little option but to introduce at least one large fish into the tank almost straightaway.

It is possible to artificially build-up your filter by putting fish food in small portions into a

Penguin tetra

fishless tank. Test for ammonia (which will peak), nitrite, then nitrates. Each should rise in turn. When the first two have peaked and fallen, do a water change to dilute nitrates and stock the first fish.

Territorial fish (usually big cichlids) will fight if one is already in possession of the tank, but that is a problem for more expert fishkeepers.

Stocking Levels

There is a surprising amount of disagreement about how many fish you can add to a tank. Some very experienced fishkeepers constantly flout all the rules and overstock. They have good filters and do lots of water changes.

A rule of thumb is one inch of fish – minus tails and appendages – for every ten square inches of surface water. So the average 3 foot by 18 inch tank can accommodate 64 inches of fish. That does not take depth into account, or how often you do water changes. However, it is dictated by the amount of oxygen in the water for each fish, which is governed by surface area.

You will see many other figures quoted, and some fish actually need to be crowded to reduce aggression, but, in general, always err on the low side.

DID YOU KNOW?

It is a good idea to deduct 10 per cent from the total volume of your tank when working out the proper dose of remedy to give. This allows for water displaced by rocks and decor in the tank.

Mollies and a platy feeding: stocking level can be determined by how much oxygen there is in the tank.

Stocking The Tank

Selecting Fish

Here are some good basic fish to look for when first stocking a normal community tank:

Neon tetras, Black widow tetras, Zebra danios, Platies and swordtails, Three spot or Blue gouramis (too big to add four at a time), Golden barbs, Cherry barbs, Corydoras catfish, small Pleco catfish, Clown loaches (when the tank has settled down). There are many more of course, but these have a good record for toughness in a community.

IDEAL CHOICE

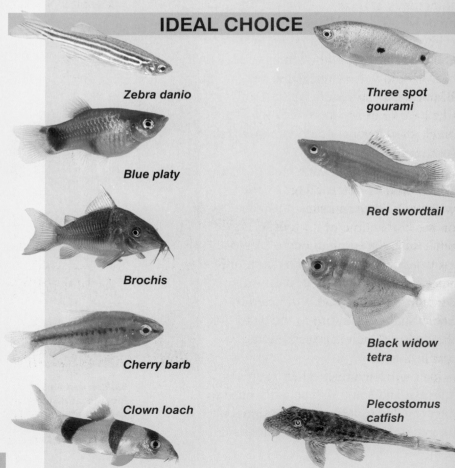

Zebra danio

Three spot gourami

Blue platy

Red swordtail

Brochis

Cherry barb

Black widow tetra

Clown loach

Plecostomus catfish

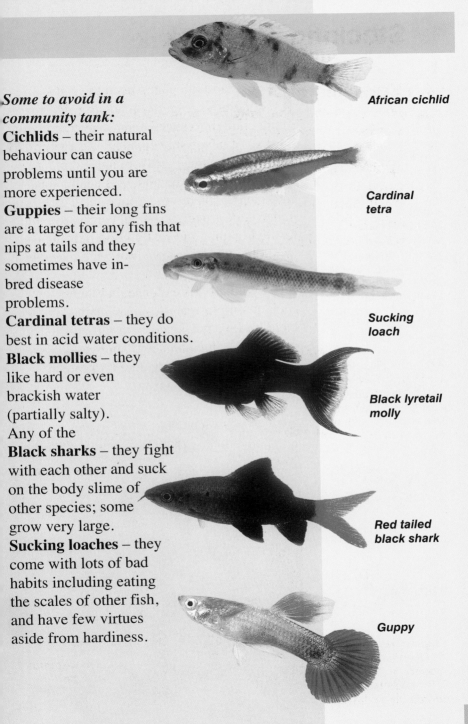

Some to avoid in a community tank:

Cichlids – their natural behaviour can cause problems until you are more experienced.

Guppies – their long fins are a target for any fish that nips at tails and they sometimes have in-bred disease problems.

Cardinal tetras – they do best in acid water conditions.

Black mollies – they like hard or even brackish water (partially salty). Any of the

Black sharks – they fight with each other and suck on the body slime of other species; some grow very large.

Sucking loaches – they come with lots of bad habits including eating the scales of other fish, and have few virtues aside from hardiness.

African cichlid

Cardinal tetra

Sucking loach

Black lyretail molly

Red tailed black shark

Guppy

Planting Your Tank

Proper aquatic plants need the right conditions to grow in aquaria. Many *are* tough enough to survive in the average tank, but lots of new fishkeepers are disappointed by the results they get from natural plants.

Briefly, for best results, you need a heating cable in the substrate, a proper iron-rich layer under your gravel, a special carbon dioxide fertilising unit, and really good lighting to promote photosynthesis (not necessarily in that order).

To avoid all this expense, beginners can stick to simple, easy-to-grow plants. These include: Java moss and Java fern, Vallis, some Amazon swords and anubias species. Some of the bulb plants like Crinum are surprisingly easy to grow.

Tiger barbs: plants will enhance your aquarium, but they need the right conditions to thrive.

For best results don't try to grow aquatic plants in an undergravel filter or even in plain gravel. You can buy a special planting medium which is full of the nutrition aquatic plants need. Following manufacturer's instructions, put a layer of this nutritionally-rich planting medium under the gravel. Alternatively, if you are using an undergravel filter, you can put the planting medium into individual pots, plant your chosen species, and cover each one with gravel to stop fish disturbing them.

You then need plenty of light to encourage the plants to grow. Fluorescent tubes have limitations. Most standard tanks are only 15 to 18 inches deep and the light that the plants need from the tubes for photosynthesis will just about reach the plants.

Deeper tanks need 'stronger' lights. Use lights recommended for plant growth, use reflectors with them and use as many as you can afford.

You are replacing the sun as far as the plants are concerned, and that's a "big ask"...

Java fern.

Amazon sword.

Vallisneria.

Routine Care

The most important part of a regular maintenance scheme is your water changes. These are essential, and without them your fish will die. Water change regimes vary a lot. A good basic routine is a 30 per cent water change every fortnight if it suits your lifestyle – or you could do as much as 50 per cent on a monthly basis. The new water dilutes pollutants in the tank, especially nitrates.

Routine water changes are essential to the well-being of your fish.

Buy a bottle of tap water conditioner and follow manufacturer's instructions. If possible, let the water reach room temperature. If not, add hot water from a kettle until it matches your tank temperature. *Always* unplug the tank before you do a water change or any other work.

Scraping the algae from the glass

Cleaning

Before you do your water change, scrub off any algae on the glass. This will fall to the bottom of the tank and can be siphoned off with any other wastes in the gravel. A gravel vacuum attachment helps to do a good job.

If you are using an internal filter, save some of the old water and rinse the sponge from your filter gently in it. Put it back in the filter, top up with the new water, and switch everything back on.

Checking

Make daily checks on the heater and filter. Check the fish out too – set aside time to watch them and look for any problems. Count them! If you feel like it, keep a log or diary of the tank.

Feeding

Feed the fish a good basic flake food. One standard feed a day will suffice – all the food should be eaten within ten minutes. Overfeeding kills more fish than starvation.

Feed a good-quality flake food.

It is true that young, growing fish need small, regular feeds all day, but the average tank with a few natural plants and algal growth may benefit from one day a week unfed.

A good flake should give your fish all the vitamins they need. Extra feeds of natural foods, once or twice a week, are a bonus. Natural foods like frozen bloodworm or safe live food like brine shrimp can be can bought in most aquatic outlets.

Beware! Overfeeding kills more fish than starvation.

You can leave your fish without food for a week or more if you go on holiday. You may want to feed them just a little more before you go in order to build them up.

It is often said that 90 per cent of disease problems can be traced to the water in the tank. Poor water conditions stress fish and damage their immune systems.

Look for early warning signs of problems.
• Fish may be gasping, perhaps at the surface.
• They make look listless with pale colours.
• They may flick or twitch.

At the first sign of ill health, test for ammonia, nitrite, nitrate and possibly pH. Even if the first three are low (and zero is the only safe measure of ammonia and nitrite), and pH is within the acceptable range (usually neutral pH 7 or just below), do a 30 per cent water change.

Some diseases are quite common and easy to treat. But remember, always ask yourself why the fish are ill. Do not just treat the symptoms and forget the problem.

DID YOU KNOW?

Old fishtank water is often high in nitrates and phosphates – making it a good free source of natural fertiliser – so use it on house plants or in the garden.

New fish do sometimes bring diseases with them. Ideally, you or the shop you buy from should quarantine them. If you have not added a new fish (or plants) recently and you suddenly get disease problems, always suspect problems with the environment in the tank.

Check if your filter and heater are working properly and do the recommended tests.

Easily identified diseases

Whitespot

White marks on your fish are common. Small, white, pinhead spots are caused by a parasite that is common on tropical fish. It is called whitespot after the cysts that form around the parasite. The disease is almost always easily treated with a shop-bought remedy.

Fungal Growths

White, fluffy, reddened areas could be wounds affected by fungus, or finrot which requires a different anti-bacterial treatment.

Angel fish.

Problem Solving

Viral Growths

If the white marks are fleshy, flexible growths – sometimes cauliflower-like growths – they are usually a fairly harmless viral growth called lymphocystis. There is no treatment, and it may disappear of its own accord.

Parasites

Parasites other than whitespot are quite rare and can usually be identified with a magnifying glass and a book on fish diseases. Leeches are occasionally seen, for instance, and are impossible to mistake. When treating for parasites (and for most bacterial diseases), treat the whole tank, not just the affected fish.

Wounds

Wounds can occasionally appear when a fish panics and swims into a rock or some other decor; they can also result from a fight in the tank. A dose of anti-bacterial treatment may help them to heal – but remember to observe the fish closely to see where the trouble is coming from.

Some medications can be harmful to Clown loaches – so read the label.

Other Conditions

Cardinal tetras.

Some conditions are very common and impossible to cure. If your fish starts wasting away, its colour fades and its body becomes bent, the problem is often 'Fish TB', an incurable bacterial disease.

Don't forget that fish can die of heart attacks, strokes, and other natural causes and that their lives in the wild may be as brief as a year. Most small fish live less than five years. If the occasional fish dies with no tell-tale signs of disease, don't panic.

In Conclusion

Keen fishkeepers are never bored. No hobby has the huge variety of fishkeeping, with, for instance, thousands of species, each with peculiar behavioural traits. Learning to tell each species apart and their scientific names is an increasingly important part of the hobby.

Many tropical fish can be bred easily, while others have never been bred and offer a lasting challenge.

Another obsession is to get their habitats exactly right, trying to match the wild as closely as possible.

Then there is the challenge of creating a superb underwater garden with all those tropical water plants.

So enjoy your fishkeeping... it's a hobby for life.

Cichlids with their behavioural problems and special habitat needs offer endless challenges.